TRI / VIA

TRI / VIA

MICHELLE NAKA PIERCE

&

VERONICA CORPUZ

Erudite Fangs · PUB LUSH
Boulder · New York · Pittsburgh

for our parents

Grateful acknowledgment to the editors of *Aufgabe, Bombay Gin, Interlope, Milk, Nieve Roja, Poets & Poems, Shiny, Southwest Symposium* and *Zapatos Rojos* (Argentina) where sections of this book first appeared, sometimes in earlier versions.

The authors would like to thank Lee Bartlett, Amy N. Corpuz, Dr. Marcelo B. Corpuz Jr., Jill Darling, Michael Friedman, Barbieo Barros Gizzi, Mike Grzymkowski, Anselm Hollo, Ross and Michiko Pierce, Chris Pusateri, and Anne Waldman.

Library of Congress Number 2002114590
ISBN 0-9726063-0-0

Cover art and frontispiece: "TRI / VIA" by Barbieo Barros Gizzi
Cover design by Norman Huelsman

Erudite Fangs
375 South 45th Street
Boulder, CO 80302

47 MacDougal Street
New York, NY 10012

PUB LUSH
714 Savannah Street #2
Pittsburgh, PA 15221
www.publush.com

Also available from Small Press Distribution
1341 Seventh Street · Berkeley, CA 94710
1-800-869-7553 · www.spdbooks.org

CONTENTS

The letter begins as an occasion. It begins as message from addresser to addressee from correspondent to correspondent.

Dear Em,

Only a few hours since you've left. Your address misplaced. Somewhere in Nagoya, perhaps. Can't sleep. Went for a walk and found a postcard too narrow to hold much of anything. I wanted to say I drew this map—up and then in. But coral stamped on the edge is a dead giveaway, which is certainly no excuse. One third of one third is trust. Our axis spinning, a tilt. You moved against the call of a bird, maybe ibis. If by *this* you imply he sleeps like an anchor most every night, surveys the diagram, worries about the mimesis of meridian, prime and otherwise, then yes, I would have to agree. No reason for concern, people suddenly make themselves scarce at times. Moving delivers the strait's disappearance. I'm never quite sure how to tell you this so it will have resonance. *Genki?* I wait for your response, which more than mock is imitation. Wondering how the equator will deviate.

Hold tight. You haven't even left yet.

Dear,

When you speak in letters marked *par avion*, you forget you are bilingual
and I am not. Confused, you remember the timetable, point to the point
of departure and say, *I've glimpsed the past looking at our future.* The legend
reads: 1931. Among all this lettering of zeroes and ones, I play the *parvenue*
recounting the pluses and minuses of balancing someone else's checkbook.
What to do? Fluctuate between *what if* and *I'm sorry*, for we are simply a
ubiquitous "they" no one seems to have an address for. The parchment
dissolves to the next scene: 1956, Buenos Aires. Again, you're talking
Greek♦ to me. When you say, "No reason for concern," you may fail to
see the integral between integers is a common denominator: zip code.

♦ By examining the origin of the word sex, we see its roots [*techne, as in art of craft, technical
skill, trickery, or trickiness*]. It is believed that the word for "love" once was identical in
meaning to "trickiness" as in the trickster, messenger, con artist, herald, inventor, god of
magic and invention♠.

♠ Q & A

1. Does this mean there is magic in the act of love?

    a. If you close your eyes, you may pull a rabbit out of a cat or a
        cat out of a carpetbag or a carpetbag from your sleeve or a
        sleeve from a tree or a tree out of a dinghy or a dinghy out
        of a compass.
    b. If you close your eyes, Prince Charming may be Sleeping
        Beauty who may be the frog who may be the woman who
        lived in a shoe who may be Robin Hood who may be
        Cinderella who may be all seven dwarfs who may be the
        rabbit who may be you.
    c. If you close your eyes, I'll be gone.
    d. If you close your eyes, everyone will swap pronouns, and you
        will be the only one wearing a slender "I" wrapped around a
        buxom "you."

2. That sex, as in the art or craft of it, requires technical skill
    or trickery?

    a. tool box
    b. magic wand, cape, and woman to be sawn in half
    c. deck of marked credit cards
    d. scatology

3. What does it take to get someone to love you?

    a. bribes
    b. cash on the nightstand
    c. matrimony
    d. a quick hand shake

4. To have sex with you?

    a. All
    b. of
    c. the
    d. above

5. In other words, what does it take to balance$^{\neq}$ long distance
    relations?

    a. musical scales
    b. pharmaceutical scales
    c. fish scales
    d. none of the above

≠ A & only A:

Strange you should ask about my equilibrium. It's been fine for months. The inner ear is a delicate thing, like a house of cards. One wrong move—flattened. As for your queries about the power of attraction*f* and assimilation, I say, *Sort all other thoughts, which form new intervals and interstices*. Notions of architecture, mapping, design: mostly gone. Genuine ionactivity, too. Kinetic contact or a contract that spurs undergoes ceaseless transformations. You interrogate the faculty that is "the organ of the ethical" in the same manner as exercise strengthens a limb. I am commonly obliged now to enter the most passive and imperious of forms—read: party, partnership, parenthood. Kinesis does sometimes seem like a way of draining a relationship of its meaning; this of course, is the constant threat of sucking out its substance, reducing it to a surface spectacle.

52 pick-up is more than a con game.

f

High speed courtship. Definition[β] of pretty, the Cheshire Cat turns to the men dressed in cards. *We all know what an ugly girl looks like.* Appalled, Alice falls asleep among the poppies while the Cat tokes hits off her powder puff. *Beauty on the inside, beauty on the out.* Pretty boys and pretty girls lining up two-by-two down the plank and out to sea. The Queen cries, *Out out, damned slut!* Down the rabbit hole and out the box, out to sea, or out of the closet: *How do you feel about girlfriends? Want 'em, need 'em, don't want 'em?* Alice wasn't looking for anything too serious, perhaps a brief foray into same-sex sex, but which sex would that be when Alice is a rabbit in a girl's suit wearing pinafores and pigtails? Alas, click your heals three times and polish up your Mary Janes—someone will whippoorwill you back, to bed you down wind or to play you down under.

[β] Such a pretty boy, such a pretty voice, such a pretty buoy—boy pretty. Such a pretty boy, such a petty void, such a petty boy—petty voice pretty. Pretty pretty hair, pretty pretty house, pretty pretty pigtails—in pity. Such a petty boy, such a pretty boy, such a pretty box—boy voiced. Such a pity boy. Such a pithy voice. Such a pretty boy—sd pity. Pity pity voice. Pithy pity boys. Pity pity voyeur—in vice. Pretty pretty vie. Pity pretty boys. Pity petty vow. Boy pretties.

Dear Em,

Try using a calculator, or better yet, an abacus in your time of crisis. Quick fingers are better tools than zeros and ones^V along a lattice. It's not that I forget, I just don't care. When I lived abroad, I'd practice my *kanji* on the sachet. Not for any reason except pride. Seems several things I do are for bragging rights. Why not try some of your own language next time to seal the deal?

Yet you got it all wrong: it's not zip codes, but sexes.

---

^{V} One and zero$^\alpha$ is all alone. Only a dome in solo. One solitary solace. A single son. A one on your shoe lace. Lonely tome in one ton. In tune soliloquy in a single tone. One inconsolable sole. Atone a solo home run and a solitary hold to monologue. *Mano à mano.* Hand in foot. Foot in mouth to mouth reception. Yoko owes no one. A wonton soup de soy lait. One and one and one baker's dozen does it.

α

Fable

"I crown thee Zero Queen."

Sir "O" his lance full of donuts whose nonchalance irked her highness. He, nonplussed, felt replete with desire: round on the sides, high in the middle. Nil from Nile to no man's land could annihilate him. Annihilated by none.

O, this nymphomaniac's necrophilia on each and every hump day. Pass. *Nil desperadum—Do not despair, pretty boys and pretty girls.*

Wanton, he chased his tail like a Zeno's paradox, wound himself into a Möbius strip. The lonely sum of nun and necrophile: love-love.

Dear Ame,

Function key, Chinese leftovers, digits, extremities, ring fingers, handyman's belt, screw, nail, iconographyχ, stain-glass windows, Sunday school, amnesia, ambivalence, hubris of the guilty, Euclidean geometry, pastiche, surmise, bookshelf, and trickery.

Letters form *arrondissements*, not genetic codes for sexuality.

χ At some other point in iconography, orange could be a question.
Or, it could be, as in Japanese folklore, a geisha exposed.

Dear Em,

Why the list? Why not just give me directions to your core or *ki*? A diagram, perhaps. You keep leaving bits of DNA—a strand of hair, shed skin, used dental floss—for clues. I'd rather have your wand and hat, the magic words, a trick box. Artifice: all of it. Maybe Plato was right. Are we just three times removed from Kansas? You say to ignore the wo/man behind the curtain, but where have I heard this before? Surely, I'm not talking just to hear myself think. Even quantum physics allows me that. Pi squared—just degrees of ardor on the axis.

Mere classifications of a house fly.

Points of view: critical, empathetic, cynical, antagonistic, devil's advocate, sympathetic, calm, compassionate, erratic, et cetera, etceteras. I find myself in the fluctuating state of inter-states at the border of Missouri and Kansas. We saw a widow. Infidelities in plural. In misery some find consensus. A bona fide form of commitment-action. Everyone thought it cowardly to have been with so many lovers. Weak, they said, for one should have plenty enough spouse in a spouse. Perhaps, in the end, the spouse had had enough[δ].

[δ] See 5% rule.

Dear,

I'm leaving you my coordinates: x, y: crossroads within the devil's handbook. Do you hear her? I do. If you've been listening long enough, I'll hear her sermons too. This mixed geography of middle Asia and interior Europe point us in improper directions. To solve the proofs: $x^2 + y^2$: a parabola's fright. Yes, hyperbolic tendencies to imply "ventricles," "arbors," "granite hands" may not determine the ordinate amounts of solipsistic blasphemy. Or maybe, I do remember. I can see your love swabbed Quaalude with unconditional hues even if you think your lunacy less motionless: frenetic buzz caught between screen and window. But we are another species: ruminate on "could." Whether you tombstone face the inferior "me" or calculate how many times we write "atlas." We've gone abroad.

Singly, you will swing a Pythagorean silence.

Dear Em,

Yes, I hear her. While the ground beneath me shakes, vertical shifts alienate the "you" from the "me." Yesterday I wondered if you'd ever collapse, fall between the domain and hypotenuse. You did—twice in eight hours must be some kind of record, changing my aura from lime-green and yellow to this. *Call in the call girl* is another way of mocking the therapeutic language of the day. I may be going in improper directions, but I haven't "solved" out to fabricated dialogue. "X, Y" or "parabola" doesn't do it for me. Snickers come because funny isn't funny anymore. Or was it ever? I understand making a name is on target; however, when did it get in the way of connubial alliances? He says no one he knew aspired for tenured relations ▸.

You left your coordinates, then just left. How solicitous.

▸ Into a sense, into the relation, into each thing into its own, each thing builds into the relation, builds a sense into each thing, a relation as if I were a singer, as if I were into each thing, into a sense of the same old song, into the same old thing, each thing into the sense, into the relation as if he were built, as if she would dissolve, as if each thing, each relation were a sense, were a song, as if we were old into each thing.

Not that you, through some malignant force, is holding on to a past "you," a you who would have written earlier, would have set aside all digressions, and in all likelihood, would have penned a more punctual letter.

Detour: *Inquiry*

Dear Betrothed; Dear Faithless:

Here is my longitude: two-pronged truths.
Latitude: strange bedfellows.

Did I strip before you and become a reptile?
Did you loosen your exterior skin?

We undid each other's coloring so as not to give
in to each other's ulterior motive.

Once I did hear anonymous say, "Health˅ is
perhaps the slowest possible rate at which one
can die." Sex, its palliative.

Did you see the beacon, where light beckoned to
idleness, and I was your favorite eulogy?

Medical History

1. What is the nature of your visit?

    a. Divine. I rarely make house calls to tell a woman she has immaculately conceived the Messiah.
    b. I followed the white rabbit.
    c. A tornado, a house, a pair of ruby shoes one size too small.
    d. I can't quite get rid of this itch.

2. How long since your last period?

    a. Two sentences ago.
    b. What's being punctual got to do with it?
    c. Three...
    d. None of the below.

3. Do you smoke?

    a. Socially.
    b. Only when I dress in tuxedos.
    c. Depends on what you mean by "smoke."
    d. Smoking is inconsequential to this investigation. The epistolists do not smoke.

4. Do you practice any of the following?

    ❏ unsafe sex   ❏ sexual taboos   ❏ laissez faire
    ❏ forgiveness   ❏ abstinence   ❏ adultery
    ❏ commitment   ❏ religious fanaticism   ❏ the piano

5. Have you experienced any of the following symptoms?

    ❏ amnesia   ❏ influenza   ❏ deafness
    ❏ bruises   ❏ tinnitus   ❏ kinesis
    ❏ aphasia   ❏ alcoholism   ❏ constipation
    ❏ cowardice   ❏ blindness   ❏ fever
    ❏ homophobia   ❏ dysmenorrhea   ❏ diarrhea

Be careful to consider the message you may be sending to your loved one when you do not take the time to look up a questionable word in the dictionary.

Dear,

We packed up the sonnets. Just Petrarchan. Now we're ready to *vas gratis*.
The transport from blank to blank (fill in any cities you like) gave me the
flu. At the mouth of truth, I asked about cross-genre bathhouses and
colossal feats. My intention did not include solicitations, but rather
subterfuge—in case my genetic codes were intercepted. Thus, the quick,
coordinate exit. Nothing personal, I guarantee.

96.5% to normal.

Dear Ame,

In your last letter you wrote, "We packed up the sonnets." In a more convenient fashion, I would never deny a couple's a-b rhyme scheme but would question whether the xx couplet or xy perform the same function$^{\varepsilon}$.

Unable to locate speed and distance simultaneously—reflection is but surfaces—all which is sprung from the mouth: a herd of hours rushing for hourly tolls. In essence, we shall see how families fill valences with non sequiturs. Data to follow.

$^{\varepsilon}$ Similar to the Heisenberg Principle of uncertainty, gender performs parlor tricks like photons or half-sawn ladies. Smoke and mirror smoke.

Dear Em,

Even if a woman penetrates a compass, she errors not in uterus—she errors in Rome. Only the raw and the cooked reveal the menace: the peel of onion and motive within a city disguised by prefix. Her manner implies frenzy there on the cellar step because the cortex traces the swerve of phosphorus blue. I see her wrestle in retina. He becomes almost all, a bridge from premise to technique. But here in the hallowed, a passport stamp to a type of Eden, we prop the density of ovaries onto turning tricks. Can her frame be a syllogism for bruises? For the masquerade of division? Indigenous as a verb, we spell the word. Proof—of our androgyny. Proof—of the complex error in combustion. I wanted to continue the kinship, just as decimals obtain simulacra. She is an engine adjacent to our nerve with the forum and senate dispersed. Clearly, had I known, I would have taken a picture of her grave, an alternate, less linear game.

In immersion we are extinct, though we still predict the outcome.

Even if one receives the compass hand—like a
newlywed in a receiving line—she hands her lover
a plea-bargain. How could one know when the
error roams? He unscrews the jar and finds the
factorial for medium-rare disguises♣.

heart attack or heart break x *skeptic or suspect* x
stand up or put down x *vows or vowels* x *commas or comas*

♣ A man stands in front of a mirror and sees a woman. A woman behind this man sees
herself. The man sees two women. The man sees himself as man as woman as reflection.
Open to translation. *Screw you*, the woman says. Inside the mirrors, there are two women,
one man, and all genders decoding the fragments to understand why they have forgotten to
remember to forget♥.

♥

He talked of a bar he had forgotten. An omniscience, the bartender said. He could barely taste the salt. The lime, forget about it. Even a sunset more citrus than Florida couldn't make them smile. While they drove to the border towns of Insomnia and Infidelity, an amnesiac waved them down. "Have you even done this before?" she asked. "I don't know," her lover replied, "—have you?" She lifted her hem and sighed. Shot glasses filled with knowledge of every conceivable something. Two diaphanous images of two tiny devils climb out of the shot glasses. "Give alms to lies," they offer "and pass the hat for liars." The beggar noticed his hands and speculated again on the name he had forgotten. *Forsythia.* He jogged after her, the smoke of a Chinatown Express bus rising to his mouth. In one breath, she could taste desert and chrome. Between the cars and lower edge of the curb, soot and the Sunday paper. An expression of a gaping mouth. "The commitments you fear," he shouted out the window, "are those of other people." Blue laws and coins in palms. They did not enter Truth or Consequences, but headed northward across the plains. After two years, he arrived at the same curb where it all began. Here, they rested the psalms inside their psalm books. Closed their eyes in fitful sleep. Minute details cross the lids: moonshine. Proofless alibis of a small invisible city, where amnesia second bests every bartender. She said, "I want to, with you. I'm in love with you." Pushes her hair back with the back of her hand. He pours the well drink over ice and pours it tall in memory of two women he had forgotten.

There are a few set rules, not of etiquette, but of the laws of self-respect. Never write anything that can be construed as sentimental.

Dear,

I have built a basilica for you[γ]. Peeling the onion layers of intellect, you tell me I have gone abroad. How can I when the chapel holds only three people? You preach to me in decimals, bituminous elegies, and poor grammar. We're insolvent now that we've given back the heathen bed, penned memoirs out of pendulums. Throwing the upper cut, you swing at the verse and cause me to bruise easily. Blue innuendoes and green prosthesis of un-nonsense. Hence, I have left the company of my cousins and have fallen sickly in love with my sister.

Ah, there it is, revealed.

[γ] Open the cunt wide but not for you. Force the nipple and bite.

Dear Em,

I never preach, never lecture, never fall into modes of banking affairs. For you to suggest that I do is retaliatory. I haven't been to "church" in decades, and "prayer" is not a mode of communication in which I partake. Talk, talk, talk about authenticity and "true" anything suspends the pendulum in a northerly direction. Do not, I warn, confuse this for the North Star. This is not symbolic of heaven, more arbitrary than fate. Nonsense, I say, is our only salvation. Look for it inside garbage cans, under sofa cushions, in lint screens. The savior is not a cloak-and-dagger, shoots-and-ladders kind of game. It's a card trick or permission to be yourself without insecurities and whining. Let this be a lesson.

Discussion of your incest to follow[η].

[η] Like two strands that compose a helix of our DNA, religious conviction and modern conventions have moved in spiral trajectories. In fact, in the hands of the *informed* ecclesiastic, we overcome difficulty with repetitive motion. For instance, by "stroking the bishop." Or, to repeat is not necessarily repetition, only a discussion on the issues of context. In correspondence it's called the fourth wall. Though invisible, it took centuries for dispatchers to actually walk through to recognize the addressees, an arc of improvisation. In a sense, penetration. In both digital and analog, the epistolists take more active roles in establishing sequence and narrative, finding the missing links between catechism and codex. Or, in playing the pawn—a failure in spirituality and faith. Checkmate.

Dear Ame,

This letter seems the easiest to write. Economic jargon and matrimony seem to go hand in hand, neck in neck. When you say "French kiss," I say "laissez-faire," though you reveal you're disinterested in sex. Interest rates[1] are soaring and dividends from a hand job decline in inverse proportions. I wouldn't consider this market failure but the results of three decades. Opportunity costs. Forgive me, I can't measure the curve of indifference, the reasons why, every morning, I can't get up, a "goodbye."

---

[1] You, who have become the entrepreneur of the caress and carcass, tell me, are you my spiritual broker or sexual accountant? What *is* the exchange rate for rubles to taboos?

alimony check or reality check, merchandise or matrimony, incest or inquest

Inside a church inside mid-morning weekday-
insides instead of pews inside the church plastic
lawn furniture instead of Bibles inside three-
ringed binders scriptures and verses inside the
polygamist's house a spouse inside spouse inside
spouse.

There is nothing in my life there is nothing there is nothing I'm ashamed of there is nothing there is nothing in my marriage there is nothing amiss there is nothing I'm ashamed of no incest no business there is no one in restraint there is nothing, I say,

"I am an apostle."

apostle or ass hole, gospel or gossip, celestial marriage or celestial being, beginning or begging

An intimate letter
has no end, has no
beginning either, has
only middle, that is
to say "middle" as
substance.

Dear,

…What happened last Thursday…I've been meaning…You're not hurt, are you?…They said it wouldn't hurt…Of course, I would believe them…Would I? I don't know…What incest?…What is wrong is your…No, no…When?…I disagree…Why can't you leave me alone?…This is sadistic…Me? *My* masochism!…They told me it wouldn't hurt$^\partial$…Yes, I believed them…[dial tone]

$^\partial$ Glass is just a state of sand, he wrote. But he knew to construct a bordello, you must first know your parts: handcuff, switch, stiletto, harness—and of course, an existential view. He assumed this site had *interiors* and *domestic spaces*. While he strongly urged the use of orange and peel together, he realized that consumers always tally up, especially when you step back a yard to earn their interest. A black space opens before the crotch. Shavings of her hair on the mantel. Her fingers never moved, and the pushpins that held them to the wall clashed with her skin tone. Yes, he could make her face from fine rice paper, even without water, and turn the dog bones into elongated hearts.

The letter begins again.

Dear Ame,

In your last phone call, I noticed your executionary style. Zip-ping! Each renunciation an arrowhead: *I always*➠, *I always, I always*. If genuflection implies authenticity, then "this bus kneels" before your better judgment that accepts pedestrian efforts over concubinal delights. I'll ride your sermon until our next stop on this chastity belt. Destination unknown, try a parable instead. In your response, you wrote: "Let this be a lesson." You put to bed your amens hiding them in tiny places big enough for a clue, an insult, a pomegranate. The station fills with arrivals and departures, embraces and farewells, printing the circumference of negative space.

➠ Always through the imagined, always into each thing, always as if I were that same old thing, that same old always, as if you were, I sd, as if I were only, he sd, that you were, she sd, only as if I were a song, the same old thing, we sd, a built song as if I were the only thing, he sd, the only thing, she sd, built into each thing, into each called upon sense, into each called upon always, as if I were, you sd, the same old song.

Dear Em,

There are pictures and pictures of rooms in semi-anonymity reflecting surface. It is midnight, and the bed stretches to reach its walls—now, a large apartment, the size of your wrist or mine. A camera at any moment flickers on the floor, makes us symbolic of combining and recombining sexual punishment. There is craft to white silk. As usual, its principle armors a craved figure, flattens your symmetry. All things considered, to index you must still point. Think in relation to the third set, where walls and vertical dimension are calm. In the end it was a kind of dust particle as massive as the complex system of verbs, only no one sees this but you.

We distinguish the events in the periphery, yet find a margin of reference$^{\lambda}$.

λ

The fact is that many theories on "relation and reference" cannot fluently be related at all because they lack a universal on which to convene and/or disband. They seem incommensurable because stated in diverse terminology, or in identical terminology with diverse signification, or similar signification with diverse outcomes, or because they are principal parts of larger systems of thought which differ in assumptions, premises, or practices. As a result, it is problematical to find where they correspond, differ, or even, what the "points" at issue are, and therefore, leave indexing in the margin or mainstream an arduous venture. Not to be confused with issues of pontification and pointillist photography or handfuls of alibis. Indeed, the partner is none other than s/he who unlearns what s/he has learned in order to know her/himself. The angst, then, of the partner, far from being the result of the world's failure to discover and appreciate her/him, arises from her/his own personal struggle to ascertain, appreciate, and finally, express the self—especially during sexual punishment.

Dear,

There are dildos and there are dildos of ruined whores in quasi-anaesthetized states. 3:06 a.m. The bed stretches to reach its walls—once a small railroad apartment the size of your narrowing ankles, now swollen with largess. A digital video camera illuminates the ceiling, renders the symbolic act of desire, merely the virtual simulacrum, as sexual crime. There's a certain craftiness to strangling a lover with red silk. The principal suspect is an armless figure. In sum, to indict the suspect, one must still point the smoking gun. To think in relation to the phone call, where shadowed floor and ceiling become none. Zero, zero. Love, forty. In the beginning it was kind of them to throw the victim into the air—light as dust particles yet enigmatic as a set of complex numbers, except no one solves this felony but you.

Dear Ame,

There is business class and there is economy, there are cattle cars and there are rummage sales, there is an emergency exit and there is commitment, there is a matchbox as memento and there is an interior motive, there are tempters and tormentors, there is exterior haste.

The letter left open on your desktop reads: *Dear, He will tell you two-ply lies on the virtues of abstinence...I will leave the tickets for you with the time tables... Creature, you dare me.*

S/he rushes to tear it from his/her hands.

There was proof and there was denial, there was a choppy motto for love, there were façades and bills and tickets, there was a clock ticking with lies rotting like waterlogged[†] wood.

†

What proof to believe and neither disbelieve when what is at stake is experiential evidence. These moments are filled with banter, casual gestures, and nods of approval. *Yes, right, I see.* Not the permanent reminder that casualty should not be confused with causality. The very opposite of kites resembling fish flying above an emptied beach. Two women—donned in large, red, woven hats— scour the shore for its question marks, listening to its insides. What they hear are sounds mimicking ocean waves. A shipwrecked box filled with the answers to all unaccountable questions. *I can't reveal my sources*, the box says. Accused by the mail carriers, the two women talk in melodic voices as if piano tuners sit inside their vocal chords. Speech systematically erratic and then, on occasion, a burst into scales—anecdotes from childhood memories, ten metaphors for feeling "in love." The couple stood laughing from inside the shipwreck buried under seaweed, coral—the bones of great white sharks that resemble kites flying high above an improbable scene.

Dear Em,

Your derisive behavior belittles not me but your intellect. For that, I can say that interior motives and cattle cars are obtuse. I'm dick-tired of this trite rummaging through my things. Do I go through your resources and fondle your credentials? Do I look for your irregular verbs and change them into gerunds? I think not. In fact, who gave you the key? I have a crick in my neck, not ever to be confused with water—stagnant or otherwise. I trusted you. I held your letters close to me and found momentum. Now I spit mock-fire in your direction, a slight southeast of east.

There are "emergencies" and then there are predicaments. There are "façades" and then there are subtext deceits. There is "exterior haste" and then there is peripheral velocity. Notice, I did not say half-past the present-day, quarter till our future.

Excursion: *Soliloquy*

It is said that the past sticks to the future, and the present is the glue we are unable to see for we are pasted upon the thin lip of envelope and seal, unable to distinguish which direction is forward or backward; thus, how do we know that we are living into the future? Perhaps, our movement forward is retraction— we retract from that inimitable destination no one wishes to reach and yet inevitably we arrive there behind ourselves or in front, alas, at the thick gluey inside of life. It is said, no one can undress oneself from this predicament of soul inside soul upon the tongue that licks and licks this life inside out. The taste of wormwood and time eking out of clocks—the wall drips seconds like a runny faucet. It is the sound of a tin pan that reminds us to stop clock-watching. It is the exultation or exhalation we unseal to unknow ourselves from this unknown.

Dear Em,

I'm in the present, looking at our past and passing the time here. Did you see her future? I caught a glimpse in the periphery, but can't get her out of my margins. I know you knew where to reference him. How to point her index finger. I can't remember: Lip stick? Lip lock? Locked up? Memories are sometimes better left unsaid and unexposed. To think, it reflects her image ℘—partly replicates; partly signifies. You ask if this *this* is a symbolic gesture.

No, a mimetic stance.

℘ Anatomical Quiz

1. *organ of the ethical*

   a. Mine?
   b. Yours?
   c. For the masquerade of division?
   d. Where have I heard this before?

2. *areola*

   a. Was it ever?
   b. Shall we have some dinner?
   c. How do you feel about girlfriends?
   d. Can her frame be a syllogism for bruises?

3. *umbilicus*

   a. Is that a chart or axis?
   b. Can our lives be marginalia?
   c. Would you?
   d. Did *you* loosen your exterior skin?

4. *la bouche*

   a. Why not try some of your language to seal the deal?
   b. Want 'em, need 'em, don't want 'em?
   c. When did it get in the way of connubial alliances?
   d. You're not hurt, are you?

5. *scatology*

   a. What incest?
   b. Do I look for your irregular verbs and change them into gerunds?
   c. Lipstick?
   d. Is six too many in bed?

Forgive you is not to forget you but to forgive me of tall drinks and weary days.
Forget you is not to forgive you, even if I sleep in flasks and long wet dreams.

Dear,

If you don't spend time actively retrieving them, the steps may become
slippery with the foul oil of disuse. In this web-tattered attic, there is
a window thickly soiled by neglect, dimly lit by previous memories and
a flash of light from present experience. The attic door opens and shuts
with a breeze of imminence. To have retrieved the steps: the minutiae we
promise not to forget: a collar curling upon itself like a viny leaf, light
reflected in the faces of tablespoons. Panting at the stairwell, trivialities
flood into a pool of crickets. Thus, no breath may resuscitate the trunks
laden with photographs, rafters hanging with decade-old calendars.
Immersed in the true fit of a slagging shell, I rest the days in their boxes.

Dear Ame,

There are only three days left or thirteen minutes until we summit each other's scalene, unknow the difference between why we've chosen this and *this*[μ]. The sign says. Whether we communicate in Morse code or algebraic ratios, we may only understand our pronouns. Co-sign the gender. Proliferating on the cuff links, there is no gendered vowel. I do know the past of the future's passing. Let's wait and see.

[μ] The sign says. The sign says this. This *this* is only a sign. Saying is thus a sign. Thus, saying, in says is only this. This is the sign. *This* is thus a this. A sign is saying no sin. A sin is thus a sign of this. A sign of thus. A sin, sign, sung a cappella this. Thus that the other and this. Thus a sign, in saying, says it is sin under the sign of Capricorn or cornucopia. This thus a sign. Thus *this*, a sin. This *that* a coping mechanism in saying this. A signal of sin in sign and say. A segment of sign. A sentiment of *this*. A say, a sign, a saying of unsung salient fists. Thus, a fist, on his *this* is signaling her to sit.

The sign says so.
So it says.

Dear Em,

I am walking and kick-dancing like a sermon whose flame is red and half insane. October's fever grass shadows the atoms dead by Darwin's tongue, but not at all like mercury. It's such a shame that hard your eyes were and any color but green. There's nothing to worry about except the madness of Buddha. You ask to hammer history into finite spaces of measures and genders. Know the difference between sign and signal regardless that you no longer drive. Again, I see the clock and its tick is louder than before. Last week, I thought I saw you walk across the parking lot into the gravel.

No boulder unturned.

Dear,

Use time signatures to outline the artifice, but don't overuse the device. Too late! Look, all the expletives have reached a new critical mass—the liturgical service has ended—and the plane I intend to land is in the middle of a field filled with useless gerunds running amok. At the periphery, woods, encroaching upon the field's definition: runway. Enter unknown. Three uses for trigonometrical modeling: horizon, speech, adultery. Read the proofs. Tangent equals red herring. Cosine equals a mutual agreement. Sine equals what the sign says. Where was I?

Dear Ame,

In the present, I recall once reading about an isosceles love triangle. Two women and one man^v or two men and one woman. They loved unilaterally until an equilateral agreement was reached. Split the week: 3-3-1 rotation. They lived until one wanted more, another helping of Friday. The sign said, *Be generous*. Gluttonous for more of more and one more man, one was left with one's vector hanging out of one's pants. As I retell you this, I feel a vague sense of *déjà vu*.

v

This *his* is
Isis or ibis
hissing sighs
and sign-language
Shit and sit
and shit
and hit
the height
of *his*
as is
as such
sissy suck
the sister
sins in this
as in a lisp
or sin
so-so
so far
high sifts
the sins
and signs
for this
is *this*
useless
sí si
so goes
his hits
and sucker
punch fits
a blast
and thus
alas no lust

Avoid large
complicated
words when a
simple one
will do. Use
lay terms.

Dear,

The betrothed and faithless engage in a tête-à-tête. I think this is the perfect place. You hang back and distrust my choice, *With horseshit everywhere?* I've always thought exchanging vows with horseshit surrounding us was apropos. Not that I think our marriage will be shit, but because I think we are jaded enough to understand that "marriage" is full of shit— an antiquated, idealized institution. A means to stand at the trough and graze with the cattle. *Then why get married?*

So we can get a bunch of shit from our friends, of course.

Enjoy one then the other enjoy one another enjoy the one and not the zero enjoy the zero not in one not in two but three enjoy the three of "we" of free "to come and go" as "we" as "we" as "something bigger" as "something better" than one of "one sum" a family fun until complete replete with "we" another one another one to wed or bed:

"All my spouses have equal privileges."

one lump or two

57

In the beginning there was one a beginning one an unspecial one in the beginning self and only the self unsanctified unspecial feeling in the beginning self in the beginning there was a beginning to follow a beginning before the latter a beginning after the first filled with sacrifice selflessness and sanctity only until one begot two thus two proclaimed,

"Sex is not the driving force in the plural marriage!"

In a revelation, two begot three and three begot more and more begot success begot from the law of heaven which begot obedience henceforth in the garden of spouses, one spouse pronounced,

"This is the way God governs us."

Points of view: insufficient, inadequate, meager, lean. It takes two to tango and many more to marry. Flat-chested and barrel-chested, they walked down the wedding aisle on Wednesday. Sanctity found in wedding vows and matrimonial panoply. She wore her wedding ring until it bore a wedlock trench around her banded ring finger. Without it, she felt as if faced to a platoon. He commandeered his squadrons and shifted his load. Rueful.

Dear Ame,

Candelabras, tulips kissing in the shape of a Gemini, bucket-seat
champagne, lip gloss, cocktails, a dubious piano player, earring and powder
puff, shoeshine, more lip gloss, bright red poppies and baby's breath, a
harp, a homophobe, a Scorpio, somebody's cousin from Murray Hill
addicted to punning, two dozen golfers dreaming of fairways, their lovers,
three dozen erring on the safe side, ten mistakes at noon, ashtrays filled to
their brims, *Someone to Watch over Me*, they shush each other until someone
trips, punch-bowl gossip, a young man too eager, preacher sauced,
lukewarm, they kiss, sixty people relax, gilded and tight-lipped, they sit.

Dear Em,

Wish you were here. Not much into astrology or astronomy, but there were two Gemini—one at Saturn's return the other a Cancer cusp. Is six too many in bed? The physics of music on the other hand, Baroque in particular, makes me cogitate. *Ah, Bach.* I could afford nothing more than an upright in those days. She looked and asked, "Why would you do that?" But I was at a loss for riposte. This sentence is about affection. That sentence is about crime. A missing key, a residued glass, and a garrote wire. Your profile, your rocking back and forth, your pauses in time. A slight turn of the left cheek.

Every sentence[π] begins with a new word. *Kitte kudasai.*

[π] To go where no woman has gone before. What Cixous would call *chaosmos.* Beyond the sole site of gender, beyond the cellular level where genes slither back and forth via osmosis. Red. In stress. Snowmelt. The polytheistic "we." To read star signs for direction as a sailor who charts the nautical night. A geneticist slits open a cell as a sailor looks up at the sky. Gemini cut in two, Cassiopeia unraveling, Orion's belt unfastened. Her twilit map ripped apart. Above her, science. Her skiff, at the edge of all circumference, rocks back and forth like profiles in conflict. Nowhere to turn around, but upon the self. She asks who to be, to become. An animist "I"? She answers, *Every sentence begins with a new world.*

Never sprinkle foreign words through a letter written in English. If hesitating between two words, always select the one of Saxon origin rather than Latin or Greek.

Dear Ame,

A bed, the size of a baby grand, five nudists trekked between wire. Sharp key, flat-chested. Struck upon the tongue, a chord sizzles into vernaculars. They speak a ripe speech spiced with tuning fork. Entering and exiting each constellation, they all Hail Bop! Coyotes and dingoes and alley cats that never sleep except to suffocate inside the keyboard, chest naked between wire.

Dear Em,

We are left, then, with a degree of cyanide humor[θ]. This is why, he said later, a man who genuflects through the usual nebula is nothing to write home about. Everyday there are more nuclei as if that somehow explains why Brecht is not our Beckett. When you visit I will play the parts of the film he liked best, as a wide action has no width. Particularly the scene where the turntable skips. Particularly the scene where the women wore yarn both sexual and arch. Can you see the center of our discourse is not parallel? That nautical behavior is overstated? That geology is the decline in the script? Or, every year we depict ourselves as convection with the dates built in. These days our sentences get cut in the middle and organize us to their architecture.

When morning came, it was not impossible.

[θ] He choked me until I was blue in the face. He started to laugh. I wasn't laughing. I was choking and coughing and pulling at his chest to get up. He sat upon my stomach, and I felt my balls were being crushed in a vice. Blue as my face. Is this my penance? Before the archangels pulled me up out of the water of my cerulean unconscious of my fated lust for my damnable lover, I came. Then, I came to. He came, too. And we laughed loudly with the poison and pleasure bluing with cyanide humor.

Dear,

Pan right. Naysayers explain the difference between Artaudian catharsis and Brecht's alienation less as a difference in atomic weight than how dirty you want to get your hands. Stop on image of window. Hidden in the file cabinet is a lubricant, a letter, and a single-sized serving of Vodka. This, for the 2:00 p.m. bell. Off screen: "Under an oak tree, I rewind the film-clipped memories—for there is indeed no other word for *memory*—of a time when I once had a child. So many ways to say *child*." Behind the door, a coat rack emptied of its duties. She wraps her sweater around her breasts. "These are breasts, and there is no other way to feel them." Bells in the many hallways ring like melodrama. "The toll for lying is a toll for dying," the protagonist says as the last image burns from overexposure and the audience heckles the projector. A spouse[P] takes a drink in the movie after the scene where the film dissolves into the scene where she takes off her clothes in fits of passion or fits of rage. Too many ways to say clichés. Suddenly, the cuckold enters the office and a fight ensues. A woman's defenestration.

When the movie ended, everything seemed possible.

ρ

People develop a power to perceive critically, so they find themselves not as a static voracity, but as voracity in process, in transformation. Hence, the spouse and the spouse-adulterer reflect simultaneously on themselves and the experiments without dichotomizing this reflection from action—a metaphorical screen upon which each projects desire-narratives in the forms of synchronous commitments—and thus, they establish bona fide forms of ethical fornication.

Too many who improvise commitment set up affairs where the results will be easily anticipated. This is antithetical to the process. They must begin with the solution of the spouse-adulterer contradiction by reconciling the contradictory poles, so that both are simultaneously spouses *and* adulterers. Here again, in this improvised set, we must take risks by breaking standard conventions. This kind of contact asks for a problem of finding and solving dialogue:

What do you think?
[Spoken with gestures, hints, innuendo to speaker with shirt buttoned down to mid-chest]

This is what tells me something more about you.
[Finger points to breastbone of previous speaker]

What are you saying?

What other way would you have me say it?

Indeed, dialogue, which breaks with the vertical patterns characteristic of banking relations, can fulfill its function as affection only if it can overcome the above contradiction. Through dialogue, the spouse and the spouse-adulterer cease to struggle. The spouse is no longer merely the one who loves, but one who is taught in dialogue with the adulterer, who in turn teaches "commitment." They become jointly responsible for the definition and process[τ].

[τ] An ad libitum mad liberal with clitoral texts—hyper and analogic.
Umbilicus cussing the umbra w/o   under wire.
Areola a la marinara,
sans morale ℧

and plenty.

☾ Lexicals

1. *arrondissements*

    a. underwear
    b. the accoutrements carried in a prostitute's "briefcase"
    c. antonym for *kitte kudasai*
    d. the plural form of *arrondissement*, a lie deceptively hidden in the multiplicitous duplicity of fiction

2. *angina*

    a. the adverbial form of *angine*: to whine or cuss through clenched teeth during anal intercourse
    b. the mother of Kanji and Genki, incestuous twins
    c. an inverted uterus
    d. M.I.A.

3. *Strega*

    a. Daughter of Em
    b. Son of Ame
    c. Lover of Em and Ame
    d. Anon

4. *Genki*

    a. the name of the suspect
    b. the name of the woman found on the ground floor
    c. the name of the film
    d. [real answer]

5. *Kanji*

    a. the dead twin of Genki; both born under the Gemini sign
    b. the scorned lover of Genki who jumped from the fourth floor window
    c. the director of *Genki*, the film
    d. the screenplay title of the sequel to *Genki*

screenplay or smoke screen, fiction or friction, hemmed in or hen pecked,
domicile or dominatrix

"We're doing it this way because it is the godly way."

Outside the marriage the outside world says we are outside the law the outside law says the marriage is illegal the outside world lays a stigma on those inside the marriage and those outside the marriage say we're spouse-swappers, swingers, burdens on society the outside world says our world is outside society:

"We do it this way *so that* we can't think.
We do it this way *because* we can't think."

drudgery or androgyny, congregation or concubinage, aesthetic or atheist,
spouse or louse or lice

The church chimes hand over our property the church rings use different last names the church and two and three to former names the church clangs be well be on welfare be wealthy for two and three to former churchgoers to give over to the church and the church rings the principal spouse is a flower the church and the brother-and-sister spouses petals the church reigns we can't be a king or kingdom with only one petal tolls the church to have three spouses one and one and one a must to enter the king's dominion the church's reins the church says one two three not third degree felony not a crime so chimes the church:

"There is no room for reality. When I left I surrendered to the idea that I would go to hell…ᵠ"

Gentile or genital, anarchic or anorexic

ᵠ More on more swingles on Carousels, single-serving packets of libido served up in an organic salad shooter cowboy-style duel. Single on single, swindled or swine.

Dear Em,

These days I starve myself. I think about heart attacks, produce, and sugar-induced comas. Commas seem indispensable, yet I deny to abuse. I've seen *Reversal of Fortune* at least a dozen times. Routine gives me refuge. Like the bells. Don't hate me cause I killed your plant. It seems I'm selfish; when I try to avoid nourishment, others near me suffer too. Somewhat like the bells. Can our lives be marginalia? Bits of fragmented words in indistinguishable scrawl on prescription pads? Could there be a way to critique with genuine praise while avoiding the backhanded "but"? Such as the bells.

In what other way would you have me say it?

Dear,

A woman's face in a passenger-side window passes us by. To pacify certain proclivities, the pastor and infidel gather at the crossroads. A woman wipes her face in the reflection of a restaurant window. Two dine on egg salad sandwiches and ask each other about the weather and "fruit." *Fine. Fine.* Church bell rings. Seasick, I try listening. Someone will decide to straighten this out[ξ]. Birds flock above the tower, migrating, for unknown purposes, toward their extinction. Tropic of Cancer. Hands wring. In the back seat, they exchange vespers. Dormant, she'll lie. All the vows evaporate: *I owe you an apology.* Spinning as if a plate, bodies buoy in the night as a straight man disappears into a diner.

[ξ] An aggregate of straight lines will mimic a curve in the same manner as flight.

One of the frequent
difficulties in composing
a letter is that your
answer is so long delayed
that you begin with an
apology, an opening
apology, an opening that
may be repellent rather
than attractive.

Dear Ame,

Whatever I do is only everything I cannot do. Living the conditional, I sift
a fork across a plate, thinking *If I could, I would* take a morsel and place it
back down. I have dreamed of you so much I'm feasting on heartburn, on
famine, on whatever I do, which is done only in the negative. You have
scribbled numbers on napkins, written me in small indecipherable lower
case letters. I can't even eat this damnable alphabet soup. It's too cold. I
have gorged myself on the digestible hours. I bed with insomnia, and your
beaux have left their stink in my sheets. You have eaten them out of me,
everything, every might-have-been. Insatiable user, you—your
indescribable uselessness. If I could say I have had enough, turn your ladle
away, but I bend to spoon morsels of quotidian from your chin, hunger on
your misgivings as you take the carving knife and slit me in thin slices for
everyone to see. O, translucent and gullible love!

gullibility or gulosity, Monday or mundane, marriage or mirage, lost or lust

Experiment: Let the ventricular language litigate between anonymous and alias. Pan left to kitchen. Dusk. Head lights flash in window. Speech left in a jar. Keys jiggle in lock. *Angina pectoris*. Door opens. The guilty susurrate like heart murmurs.

How was your day?

I'm home, too.

Fine. Yours?

What did you do?

Busy, terribly busy.

Something[φ].

Something?

Yes, mine too.

Terribly.

Yes, don't we all.

Everyday.

True, don't you think?

Would've never thought.

I agree.

Pleasant.

[φ] If the "something" behind everything else forces semantics, then and only then, will the informant understand that the genders involved in a discussion may not have "shared basic assumptions." Therefore, instead of using Socratic methods of questioning to help partners find their own answers, they *inform* the partners (husbands, wives, lovers—same sex or not—androgynous duos, *ménages à trois*, or menageries) about the theatrical climate and rhetoric. Informing does not imply sneaking in banking models of communication, just sneaking in late at night. Irrefutably, a structured improvisational affair is seen as risky business. However, anyone involved with improvisational sex must be willing to risk exposure. Risk is concomitant to lateral fucking. The staged and known structures allow for the unstaged and unknown to surface in their interaction, and as a result, into their intercourse: verbal, physical, and mental.

Shall we have dinner?

Will you join me?

Everyday.

Yes, each and every.

More or less.

Shall we eat?

Shortly.

Tomorrow.

Maybe tomorrow.

I suppose tomorrow. Or Saturday.

Yes, looks like rain.

More tomorrow.

They say.

I'll have another helping.

More of more.

In a manner of speaking, *this* happens often.

You don't say.

That's why I don't tell you anything.

All the same.

Aren't you going to say anything?

—

Dear Em,

It is two days after the holiday—the day we climbed the Swing Buddha, to put the mouth to, to subtract, and total the sentence. But there are few signs, if any, of the affair, which from a distance reminds us of crows. We wander into virtual nouns, leave the week behind, and find fraud. The smell of suspect on the rise lets the currency in other countries triple in value, save the market of artistic map folding on the decline. Our hands offered us a kind of syntax that day, an intricate diagram of mountains and mesas, the heat of the valley rising off our fingertips. This is to say that whatever the ruse, the response arrives in mere geography.

Somewhere between a bottle of Strega and this▶ꓭ last note.

▶ꓭ   *this, in*

Always, you sd, the only thing called upon, we sd, the only thing called upon were hands, I sd, the only thing called upon, we sd, hands called upon, the only thing called upon were hands, as if I were the called upon, you sd, as if we were the thing, I sd, as if you were the same old song, the same old thing, the same old always called upon thing, I sd, as if I were, you sd, the thing called upon.

Dear,

I don't know much about geography—nor do I know what a slide rule is for—but I do know that the shortest distance between two lines is an *aéroplane*: airborne, metallic sibilance, whirring red. A communiqué useful, untrustworthy as my cartographer's mistress. Once solved, the location is a green-gray X-marks-the-spot of an almost forgotten place populated by interior city-dwellers—however relentless in their seasonal rage, they destroy the infinitesimal *topos* of unknowns. Remind me again of what I am speaking, of what I have chosen to forget. Dishonorable, disoriented, *la bouche* is the newest location, but the city-dwellers have colonized the wagging tongue!

Dear Em,

Your letter is geographically challenged. My response is made of thought
possibly so.

The palm's hysterical bark suddenly teacups into September. So many
splendid vistas if need be. The tumbling Madame. Maggots summary
fucked. Why do women who use cigars breathe a history lesson? In the
neck of woven jade, drapery lids & sexual privileges stand erect. My sax
clutches her wounds, but he is cold & cannot hide his sex. In this instance
you could braid vibrations though you choose to diffuse alarm. Whereas
the golden cheek embraces a jar of ointment. Myth drag-assed & scarred
lip-to-lip with Manhattan. The correspondence isn't necessarily sent—
sometimes it just disappears. 10:30 & the telegrams have gone insane.

The aim of the
letter is merely to
bring in a personal
hyphen between
the person writing
and the person
written to.

Poem as letter as email as collaboration as conversation as discourse as interchange as collection as accumulation as copious pages as manuscript as so on and so forth as et cetera as trivium as effluvium of minutiae as the usual details as in trivia as in *TRI* / *VIA* as in three ways as in *ménage à trois* as in Hermes in bed or Hermes at the crossroads as in point of exchange as in, dare say, commerce as thief as trickster as technology as annotation as footnote as distance as expansive gaps as suspension of time as interval or hiatus or procrastination as sabbatical as Sabbath as sin or pathos or relations as in sex[es] as in playing footsie in an affair as inter[sexed]actions as dialogues as epistles as in *this* as dispatch.